V&A Pattern
Walter Crane

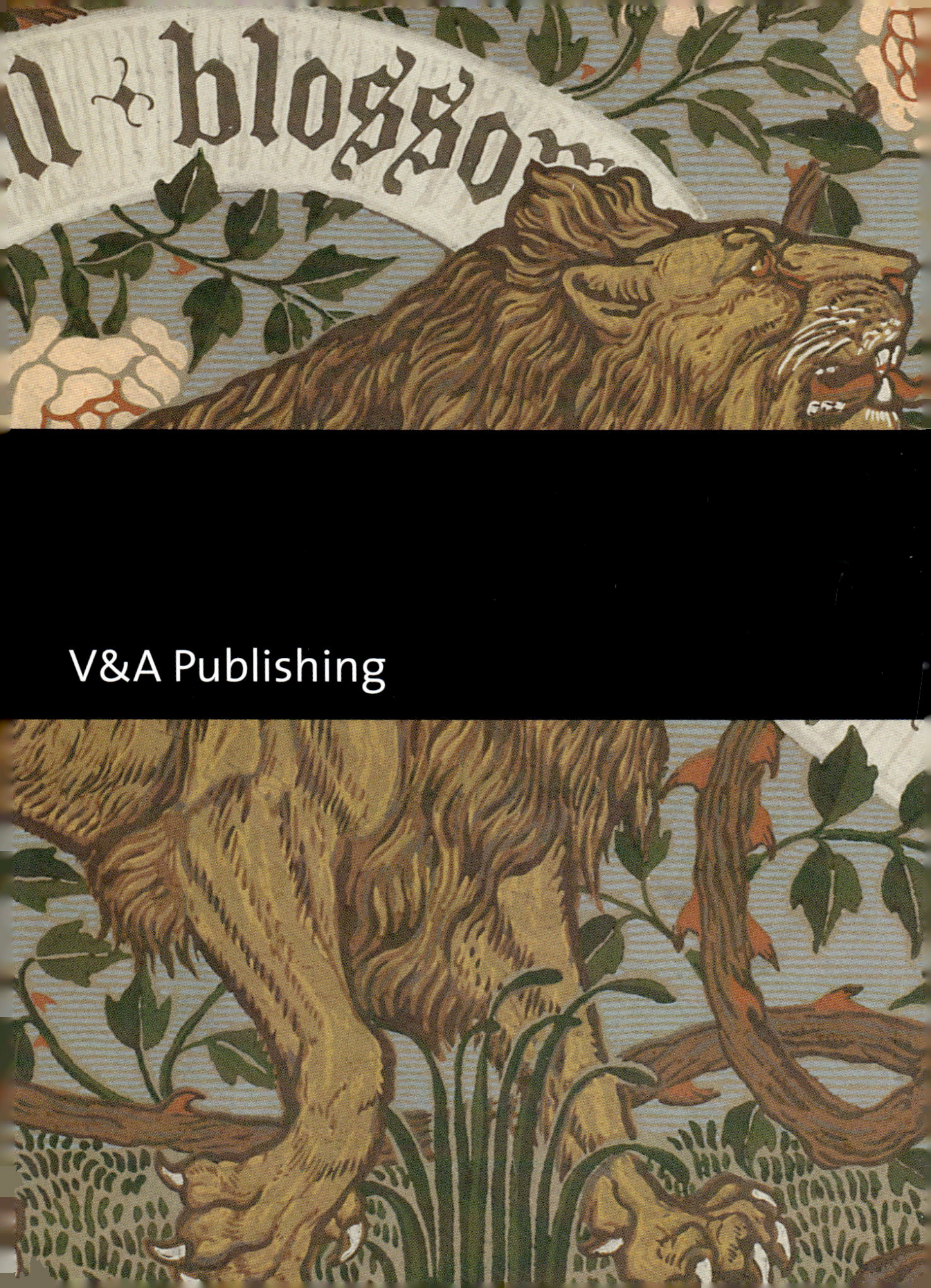

V&A Publishing

V&A Pattern

Walter Crane

First published by V&A Publishing, 2011
V&A Publishing
Victoria and Albert Museum
South Kensington
London SW7 2RL

Distributed in North America by Harry N. Abrams, Inc., New York

ISBN 978 1 85177 637 5
Library of Congress Control Number 2010937387

10 9 8 7 6 5 4 3 2 1
2015 2014 2013 2012 2011

A catalogue record for this book is available
from the British Library.

Series Art Direction: Rose
Design: TurnbullGrey www.turnbullgrey.co.uk

Front cover (A):
Walter Crane/Jeffrey & Co. *Francesca*, wallpaper. Woodblock print on paper. UK, 1902
(V&A: E.1838–1934)
Pages 2–3 (B):
Walter Crane/Jeffrey & Co. *Lion and Dove*, frieze. Woodblock print on paper. UK, 1900
(V&A: E.1759–1914)
Page 6 (C):
Walter Crane/Edmund Potter & Co. *The British Empire*, furnishing fabric. Roller-printed cotton. UK, 1887
(V&A: Circ.837–1967, Given by JWF Morton)
Page 11 (D):
Walter Crane/Jeffrey & Co. *Peacock Garden*, wallpaper. Woodblock print on paper. UK, 1889
(V&A: E.1762–1914)
Pages 78–9 (E):
Walter Crane/Jeffrey & Co. *Dove and Daisy*, frieze. Woodblock print on paper. UK, 1876
(V&A: E.1886–1934)

Letters (in brackets) refer to the file name of the images on the accompanying disc.

Printed in China

V&A Publishing
Victoria and Albert Museum
South Kensington
London SW7 2RL
www.vandabooks.com

V&A Pattern

Each *V&A Pattern* book is an introduction to the Victoria and Albert Museum's extraordinarily diverse collection. The museum has more than three million designs for textiles, decorations, wallpapers and prints; some well-known, others less so. This series explores pattern-making in all its forms, across the world and through the centuries. The books are intended to be both beautiful and useful – showing patterns to enjoy in their own right and as inspiration for new design.

V&A Pattern presents the greatest names and styles in design, while also highlighting the work of anonymous draughtsmen and designers, often working unacknowledged in workshops, studios and factories, and responsible for designs of aesthetic originality and technical virtuosity. Many of the most interesting and imaginative designs are seen too rarely. *V&A Pattern* gathers details from our best objects and hidden treasures from pattern books, swatch books, company archives, design records and catalogues to form a fascinating introduction to the variety and beauty of pattern at the V&A.

The compact disc at the back of each book invites you to appreciate the ingenuity of the designs, and the endless possibilities for their application. To use the images professionally, you need permission from V&A Images, as the V&A controls – on behalf of others – the rights held in its books and CD-Roms. *V&A Pattern* can only ever be a tiny selection of the designs available at www.vandaimages.com. We see requests to use images as an opportunity to help us to develop and improve our licensing programme – and for us to let you know about images you may not have found elsewhere.

SOUTH AFRICA
AUSTRALIA
INDIA
BRITANNIA

Walter Crane

Esmé Whittaker

When Walter Crane (1845–1915) delivered his first design to the wallpaper manufacturer Jeffrey & Co. in 1875, Metford Warner, the director of the London-based firm, received it with mixed emotions. He would later recall 'with what delight I hailed the design and the pang I felt when I considered how I was to try and reproduce it'. The collaboration between Walter Crane and Jeffrey & Co. exemplified an emerging trend in the second half of the nineteenth century whereby manufacturers employed leading artists and architects, such as EW Godwin, William Burges and Bruce Talbert, to improve design standards and produce 'art furnishings'. As a designer of wallpapers and textiles, Walter Crane had to carefully balance his desire to create beautiful and original patterns against the practicalities of production and the social expectations that dictated their use within the home.

The wallpaper pattern (V&A: E.42–1971) causing Warner both delight and anxiety was for a children's nursery. Noticing a gap in the market – few nursery wallpapers were being produced in the early 1870s – Warner commissioned Crane because of his growing reputation as an illustrator of children's books. Further commissions from Jeffrey & Co. would follow and Crane became well known for wallpaper designs depicting enchanting scenes based upon fairytales and nursery rhymes, including *Sleeping Beauty* (plate 3) and *The House That Jack Built* (plate 6). When he moved beyond the nursery to create wallpapers and textiles for other rooms, Crane continued, with greater subtlety, to take inspiration from myth, poetry and literature. The wallpaper *La Margarete* (plates 9 and 10) was inspired by one of Chaucer's poems, while *Woodnotes* (plate 61) took a Shakespearean passage as the basis for its design. Crane believed that pattern and poetry shared a common purpose; to bring a touch of joy and beauty to everyday life.

Some critics questioned whether Crane's patterns were more illustrative than decorative and therefore better suited to picture books than home interiors. There were concerns that while his designs were suitable for the nursery, where they would encourage 'liveliness' and 'merriment', they were too assertive for the remainder of the house, where the decoration should be reposeful and unobtrusive. Crane countered such criticism by keeping the purpose and eventual placement of his patterns at the forefront of his mind and producing wallpapers that complemented their intended rooms.

Crane designed coordinating papers that, as was fashionable in the 1870s and 1880s, divided the wall into three sections. For example, *La Margarete* was intended to act as 'filling' on the main portion of the wall between the *Lily and Dove* dado paper (plate 54), covering the lower portion of the wall, and either the *Alcestis* or the *Dove and Daisy* frieze (plate 53, pp.78–9), sitting close to the ceiling. He even designed a coordinating ceiling paper that incorporated the dove motif (plate 52). Through the repetition of motifs and careful colour harmonies, Crane aimed to create complete decorative schemes that avoided the patchwork of conflicting pattern and colour typical of cluttered mid-Victorian interiors.

As wallpapers and rugs are intended to cover flat surfaces, Crane believed their patterns should have a 'flatness of treatment' so he adapted, rather than imitated, the natural forms of flowers and foliage, working them into systematic pattern repeats that nonetheless retained the freshness and vitality of their sources. For hand-printed wallpapers, the repeat was limited by the size of the printing block, whereas for carpets, including *Daffodil and Bluebell* (plates 21 and 22), the design had to allow for the texture of the pile.

Crane took inspiration for his pattern designs from a wide range of sources: the delicate blossoms of the *Almond Blossom and Swallow* frieze (plate 30) reveal the influence of Japanese art; thirteenth-century Sicilian silks inspired the *Corona Vitae* wallpaper (plate 42); and an interest in medieval heraldry resulted in *National* (plates 65 and 66). Crane also used animals and human figures to enrich and enliven his flower and foliage patterns. From the slumbering princess of *Sleeping Beauty* to the jousting knights of *England and France* (plate 63), he transformed humans into pattern. In explaining such treatment, he pointed to historical precedents for the conventionalization of the figure and the practice of positioning the body within an architectural frame, as found in the stonework of Gothic cathedrals and the pediments of classical temples. *The House that Jack Built* with its depiction of monks seated in Gothic niches and the *Alcestis* frieze with its sequence of classically draped figures illustrate this technique.

The wide range of sources that influenced Crane indicates his position at the centre of the overlapping Aesthetic and Arts and Crafts movements. While Aesthetic artists sought a new kind of beauty based upon the formal qualities of line and colour, rather than religious or moral content, and looked to Japan and Ancient Greece for inspiration, socially motivated Arts and Crafts artists took a romantic view of medieval art, considering it the product of a simpler society. Crane's use of the human figure as an element of pattern design, however, was highly unusual, and distinguished his wallpapers and textiles from those produced by contemporaries Lewis F Day and William Morris. Metford Warner recalled how in the early days of their working relationship 'Mr Crane warned me that I must not ask him to design in any given style'. The variety and richness of Walter Crane's patterns for Jeffrey & Co. indicate that Warner followed the designer's advice, allowing Crane the freedom to express his individuality and imagination.

1
Walter Crane/Jeffrey & Co.
Rose and Cupid, dado paper. Woodblock print on paper. UK, 1881 (V&A: E.5089–1919)

2
Walter Crane/Jeffrey & Co.
Briar Rose, wallpaper. Woodblock print on paper. UK, 1880 (V&A: E.5090–1919)

3
Walter Crane/Jeffrey & Co.
Sleeping Beauty, wallpaper. Machine print on paper. UK, 1879 (V&A: E.60–1968, Given by Mrs Elisabet Hidemark)

4
Walter Crane/Jeffrey & Co.
Nursery Rhymes, wallpaper. Machine print on paper. UK, 1876 (V&A: E.42A–1971, Given by Mr Roger HM Warner)

5
Walter Crane/Jeffrey & Co.
Fairy Garden, wallpaper. Machine print on paper. UK, 1890 (V&A: E.4043–1915)

6
Walter Crane/Jeffrey & Co.
The House That Jack Built, wallpaper. Machine print on paper. UK, 1886 (V&A: E.2292–1931)

7
Walter Crane/Lightbown, Aspinall & Co.
Mistress Mary, frieze. Machine print on paper. UK, 1903 (V&A: E.5161–1919)

8
Walter Crane/Jeffrey & Co.
Girls Skipping, frieze. Woodblock print on paper. UK, 1880 (V&A: E.4030–1915)

9
Walter Crane/Jeffrey & Co.
La Margarete, wallpaper (see also pl.10). Gouache on paper. UK, 1876 (V&A: E.18–1945)

10
Walter Crane/Jeffrey & Co.
La Margarete, wallpaper (see also pl.9). Gouache on paper. UK, 1876 (V&A: E.2322–1932)

11
Walter Crane/Jeffrey & Co.
Rosamund, frieze. Woodblock print on paper. UK, 1908 (V&A: E.1847–1934)

12
Walter Crane/Jeffrey & Co.
Saxon, wallpaper. Woodblock print on paper. UK, 1909 (V&A: E.2324–1932)

13
Walter Crane/Jeffrey & Co.
Rosamund, wallpaper. Woodblock print on paper. UK, 1908 (V&A: E.2312–1932)

14
Walter Crane/Jeffrey & Co.
Rose Bush, wallpaper. Woodblock print on paper. UK, 1900 (V&A: E.2229–1913)

15
Walter Crane/Jeffrey & Co.
Oak, wallpaper. Woodblock print on paper. UK, 1904 (V&A: E.5057–1919)

16
Walter Crane/Jeffrey & Co.
Lily and Rose, wallpaper. Woodblock print on paper. UK, 1894 (V&A: E.5164–1919)

17
Walter Crane/Jeffrey & Co.
The Formal Garden, wallpaper (see also pl.18). Woodblock print on paper. UK, 1904 (V&A: E.1840–1934)

18
Walter Crane/Jeffrey & Co.
The Formal Garden, wallpaper (see also pl.17). Woodblock print on paper. UK, 1904 (V&A: E.5104–1919)

19
Walter Crane/Jeffrey & Co.
Day Lily, wallpaper (see also pl.20). Woodblock print on paper. UK, 1897 (V&A: E.5151–1919)

20
Walter Crane/Jeffrey & Co.
Day Lily, wallpaper (see also pl.19). Woodblock print on paper. UK, 1897 (V&A: E.2317–1932)

21
Walter Crane
Design for *Daffodil and Bluebell* carpet (see also pl.22). Pencil and watercolour on paper. UK, *c.*1895
(V&A: E.2325–1920)

22
Walter Crane/James Templeton & Co.
Daffodil and Bluebell, carpet sample (see also pl.21). Wool and jute looped pile. UK, *c.*1896
(V&A: T.99–1953)

23
Walter Crane/Jeffrey & Co.
Lily, wallpaper. Woodblock print on paper. UK, 1900 (V&A: E.2326–1932)

24
Walter Crane
Design for *Iris* printed cotton. Watercolour on paper. UK, 1903 (V&A: E.2328–1920)

25
Walter Crane/Jeffrey & Co.
Seed and Flower, wallpaper. Woodblock print on paper. UK, 1893 (V&A: E.4033–1915)

26
Walter Crane/Jeffrey & Co.
Meadow Flowers, wallpaper (see also pl.27). Woodblock print on paper. UK, 1896 (V&A: E.5088–1919)

27
Walter Crane/Jeffrey & Co.
Meadow Flowers, wallpaper (see also pl.26). Woodblock print on paper. UK, 1896 (V&A: E.5085–1919)

28
Walter Crane/Jeffrey & Co.
May Tree, frieze. Woodblock print on paper. UK, 1896 (V&A: E.5113–1919)

29
Walter Crane/Jeffrey & Co.
Wallpaper. Woodblock print on paper. UK, *c*.1878 (V&A: E.4021–1915)

30
Walter Crane/Jeffrey & Co.
Almond Blossom and Swallow, frieze. Woodblock print on paper. UK, 1878 (V&A: E.4037–1915)

31
Walter Crane
Design for *Almond Blossom and Wallflower* wallpaper. Bodycolour on paper. UK, 1878 (V&A: E.641–1952)

32
Walter Crane/Jeffrey & Co.
Frieze. Woodblock print on paper. UK, c.1875 (V&A: E.1856–1934)

33
Walter Crane/Jeffrey & Co.
Billow, wallpaper. Woodblock print on paper. UK, 1879 (V&A: E.4024–1915)

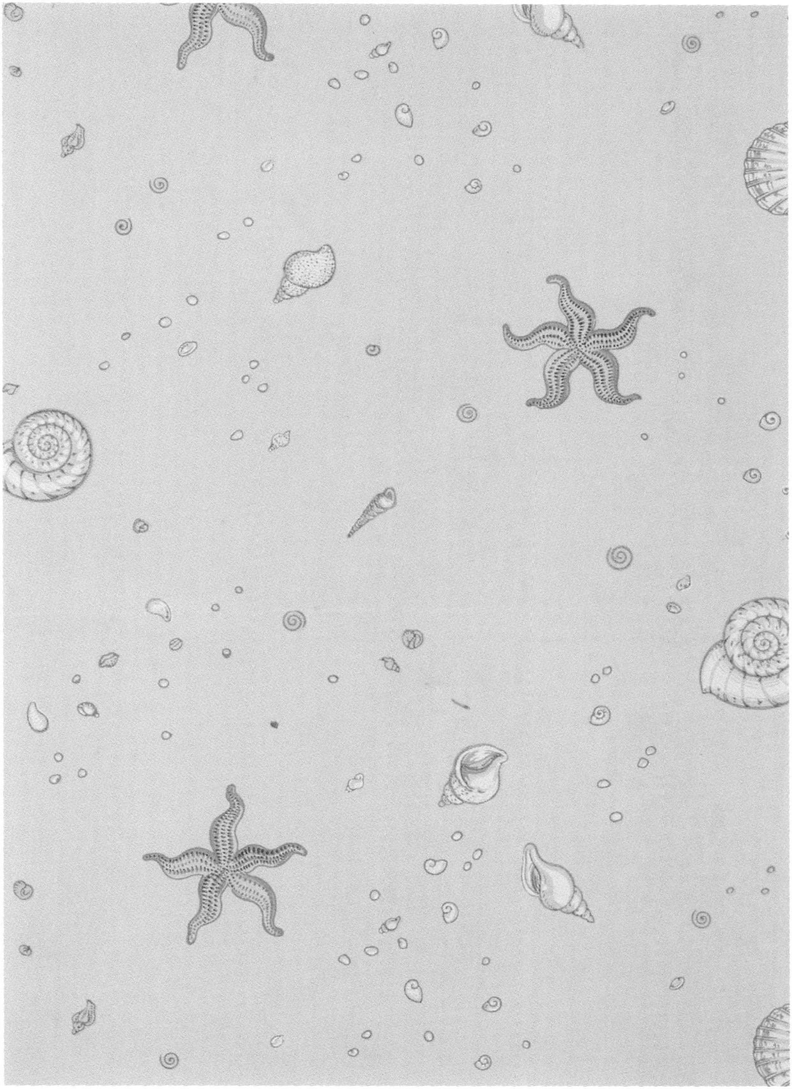

34
Walter Crane/Jeffrey & Co.
Dado paper. Woodblock print on paper. UK, 1879 (V&A: E.4029–1915)

35
Walter Crane/Jeffrey & Co.
Fish in a Roundel, dado paper. Woodblock print on paper. UK, 1878 (V&A: E.4031–1915)

36
Walter Crane/Jeffrey & Co.
Awakening Day, wallpaper. Woodblock print on paper. UK, 1880 (V&A: E.5160–1919)

37
Walter Crane/Jeffrey & Co.
Vineyard, wallpaper. Woodblock print on paper. UK, 1912 (V&A: E.1767–1914)

38
Walter Crane/Jeffrey & Co.
Peacocks and Amorini, wallpaper. Woodblock print on paper. UK, 1877 (V&A: E.4047–1915)

39
Walter Crane/Jeffrey & Co.
Plumes, wallpaper (see also pl.40). Woodblock print on paper. UK, 1893 (V&A: E.4020–1915)

40
Walter Crane/Jeffrey & Co.
Plumes, wallpaper (see also pl.39). Woodblock print on paper. UK, 1893 (V&A: E.4019–1915)

41
Walter Crane/Jeffrey & Co.
Fig and Peacock, wallpaper. Woodblock print on paper. UK, *c.*1895 (V&A: E.266–1949)

42
Walter Crane/Jeffrey & Co.
Corona Vitae, wallpaper. Woodblock print on paper. UK, 1890 (V&A: E.4046–1915)

43
Walter Crane/Jeffrey & Co.
Orange Tree, wallpaper. Woodblock print on paper. UK, 1902 (V&A: E.5139–1919)

44
Walter Crane/Jeffrey & Co.
Cockatoo and Pomegranate, wallpaper. Woodblock print on paper. UK, 1899 (V&A: E.2320–1932)

45
Walter Crane/Jeffrey & Co.
Singing Bird, wallpaper. Woodblock print on paper. UK, 1893 (V&A: E.4044–1915)

46
Walter Crane
Design for a stencil. Watercolour on paper. UK, *c.*1900. (V&A: E.2386–1920)

47
Walter Crane/Jeffrey & Co.
Iris and Kingfisher, wallpaper. Woodblock print on paper. UK, 1877 (V&A: E.4035–1915)

48
Walter Crane/Jeffrey & Co.
Frieze. Woodblock print on paper. UK, 1877 (V&A: E.1866–1934)

49
Walter Crane
Design for *Swan, Rush and Iris* dado paper. Bodycolour on paper. UK, 1875 (V&A: E.17–1945)

50
Walter Crane/Jeffrey & Co.
Dado paper. Woodblock print on paper. UK, 1877 (V&A: E.1849–1934)

51
Walter Crane/Jeffrey & Co.
Frieze. Woodblock print on paper. UK, 1911 (V&A: E.5133–1919)

52
Walter Crane/Jeffrey & Co.
Dove, ceiling paper. Woodblock print on paper. UK, 1876 (V&A: E.5115–1919)

53
Walter Crane/Jeffrey & Co.
Alcestis, frieze. Woodblock print on paper. UK, 1876 (V&A: E.1843–1934)

54
Walter Crane/Jeffrey & Co.
Lily and Dove, dado paper. Woodblock print on paper. UK, 1876 (V&A: E.4027–1915)

55
Walter Crane/Jeffrey & Co.
Myrtle Wreath, wallpaper. Woodblock print on paper. UK, 1904 (V&A: E.5109–1919)

56
Walter Crane/Jeffrey & Co.
Dawn, wallpaper. Woodblock print on paper. UK, 1902 (V&A: E.2314–1932)

57
Walter Crane/Jeffrey & Co.
Four Winds, ceiling paper. Woodblock print on paper. UK, 1890 (V&A: E.4049–1915)

58
Walter Crane/Jeffrey & Co.
Corona Vitae, frieze. Woodblock print on paper. UK, 1890 (V&A: E.4041–1915)

59
Walter Crane/Jeffrey & Co.
The Golden Age, wallpaper. Woodblock print on paper. UK, 1887 (V&A: E.2319–1932)

60
Walter Crane/Jeffrey & Co.
Peacocks and Amorini, wallpaper. Woodblock print on paper. UK, 1877 (V&A: E.4048–1915)

61
Walter Crane/Jeffrey & Co.
Woodnotes, wallpaper. Woodblock print on paper. UK, 1886 (V&A: E.1766–1914)

62
Walter Crane/Jeffrey & Co.
Deer and Rabbits, frieze. Woodblock print on paper. UK, 1887 (V&A: E.4040–1915)

63
Walter Crane/Warner & Sons
England and France, furnishing fabric. Woven wool and cotton. UK, 1908
(V&A: T.192–1972)

64
Walter Crane
Design for *The National Arms of England, Scotland and Ireland* textile. Pencil and watercolour on paper. UK, *c*.1902 (V&A: D.168–1903)

65
Walter Crane/Jeffrey & Co.
National, wallpaper (see also pl. 66). Woodblock print on paper. UK, 1897 (V&A: E.5118–1919)

66
Walter Crane/Jeffrey & Co.
National, wallpaper (see also pl. 65). Woodblock print on paper. UK, 1897 (V&A: E.5122–1919)

Further Reading

Smith, Greg and Hyde, Sarah, eds.
Walter Crane, 1845–1915:
Artist, Designer and Socialist
London, 1989

Spencer, Isobel
Walter Crane
London, 1975

O'Neill, Morna
'Art and Labour's Cause is One':
Walter Crane and Manchester, 1880–1915
Manchester, 2008

Digital Images

The patterns reproduced in this book are stored on the accompanying compact disc as jpeg files (at approximately A5-size, 300 dpi). You should be able to open them, and manipulate them, direct from the CD-ROM in most modern image software (on Windows or Mac platforms), and no installation should be required (although we, as publishers, cannot guarantee absolutely that the disk will be accessible for every computer).

Instructions for tracing and tiling the images will be found with the documentation for your software.

The names of the files correspond to the V&A inventory numbers of the images.